## My Heart's Desire

There's a country-like place in the mountains
Far away from the city mills
No place is so dear to my childhood
As the house way up on the hill

There were all kinds of fruits and berries
And flowers blooming day after day
And the birds all singing so sweetly
While on the branches of trees they'd sway

There was a big rock in front of the house
Where I sat and ate my dinner each day
From there I could see all the smoke stacks
In the city so far away

I used to help my grandfather feed chickens
And pick apples and pears off the trees
He owned acres and acres of woodland
How I wish it belonged to me

If I'm able to fill my "heart's desire"
Even if I'm old and gray
I'll go back to the house on the hilltop
Yes, forever and a day

By Joan Rissmeyer

Also by Maryann Makekau

When Your Teacher Has Cancer
When Your Mom Has Cancer
When Mom's Cancer Doesn't Go Away
When Your Dad Goes to War
When Your Mom Goes to War

Also by Bob Deits

Life after Loss

# When Your Grandma Forgets

## Helping Children Cope with Alzheimer's And Beyond

Maryann Makekau and Bob Deits, M.Th.

Artistry by 20/30north Studios

With a Foreword by

Pierre N. Tariot, MD

"Be completely humble and gentle; be patient, bearing with one another in love."
- Ephesians 4:2

Copyright 2012, 2020 by Makekau
Artistry: 20/30north Studios
Copy Editing: Amaryllis Sánchez Wohlever MD

All rights reserved. No part of this publication may be reproduced, stored in a retrieval system, or transmitted, in any form or by any means, electronic, mechanical, photocopying, recording or otherwise, without the prior written permission of the author/publisher. Printed in the United States of America.

For information, address:
Hope Matters Productions, Inc.
Attn: Maryann Makekau
PO Box 2021
Fort Walton Beach, FL 32549
www.becausehopematters.com

Set in Kristen ITC 12 point. Includes references.

When Your Grandma Forgets: Helping Children Cope with Alzheimer's and Beyond: Library of Congress Preassigned Control Number 2012904599.
Makekau

ISBN-13: 9780982660133
ISBN-10: 0-9826601-3-8


Note: The information in this book is true and complete to the best of our knowledge. This book is intended only as an informative guide for those wishing to know more about issues related to Alzheimer's disease. In no way is this book intended to replace, countermand or conflict with the advice given to you by your own physician. The ultimate decision concerning care should be made between you and your doctor. We strongly recommend you follow his or her advice. Information in this book is general and is offered with no guarantees on the part of the author or publisher. The author and publisher disclaim all liability in connection with use of this book.

# FOREWORD

Why read a book to or with your children about an illness with an unusual name? They might say, "What does it have to do with me? It would be more fun to read a Little Pink Book!"

Here's why. A lot of our Grandmas and Grandpas will get Alzheimer's. It used to be rare, but it is much more common now. In the old days, people did not live as long as many do now. It turns out that being lucky enough to live a long time means the not-so-good luck of having an increased chance of getting Alzheimer's, since advanced age is one of the biggest risk factors for Alzheimer's.

This book will help your children (and you!) understand this illness with an unusual name. It will help them learn some basic facts: that it is a disease that can steal memories from people and gradually make them look and act differently from their usual selves. It will help them understand Grandma better, even if she has a new illness that affects how she thinks, talks, and acts. It will help them (and you) understand how to give her what she needs most: to still be Grandma. Just because a thief stole her memory does not mean that she will disappear overnight. She really is and always will be Grandma, just different.

Reading this book will show you and your children that you can feel good about giving hope and help to one of the most important people in the world. From recording and reusing "keeper" experiences to bringing humor into the picture (after all, it is better perhaps to laugh than to cry sometimes!), to allowing grief to unfold, your children can experience a new sense of understanding and mastery that can afford them, and Grandma, renewed hope and joy.

While you learn together, we doctors and scientists will work hard to find medicines to stop Alzheimer's in its tracks. And, who knows? Maybe our efforts to delay its onset or prevent it altogether will work. Wish us well. In the meantime, I'll know that Grandma is in good hands.

Pierre N. Tariot MD,<br>
Internal Medicine and Geriatric Psychiatry<br>
Director of the Banner Alzheimer's Institute

# DEDICATION

When Alzheimer's disease invades a home, it begins to transform steadfast memories into fleeting snapshots. Birthday cards go out without the usual note from Grandma—and she didn't even sign her name. A trip to a favorite restaurant proves too much when the server hands her the bill—and Grandma's face blushes with confusion. To-do lists that were once easily followed must now be broken down into single steps—to be repeated again and again.

This isn't the Grandma you've always known—this is Grandma with Alzheimer's disease taking over her life. It has stolen her reign as "queen" of Scrabble. It's reduced her poetic brilliance to a muddle. As the disease progresses, its effect on her loved ones is becoming painfully obvious. When Your Grandma Forgets is dedicated to my mother, Joan, to her five children and to her nine grandchildren who lovingly adapt no matter what Alzheimer's disease steals.

To all those who bravely shared their walk through forgetfulness with me: Ruthie, Donna, Karen, Ernie, Kathy, Rhoda, Charlie, Vi, and my father, Ernest. To Chuck: my sweet companion in all life's ventures. To my illustrator, Derek, at 20/30north Studios; thank you for bringing the whimsical into another very difficult topic. Thanks to my exceptional copy editor and translator, Mari. Thanks also to my classroom reviewers, Vicki and Lily.

To Bob: my deepest gratitude for co-writing this work of the heart; and to his life-long love, June, for her exemplary courage to "punch through the cloud" of confusion and fear. To every reader: may you be blessed with hope, faith and love—the gifts that remain despite all odds.

Maryann Makekau

# DEDICATION

I first saw the effects of Alzheimer's disease up close and personal in my wife's father, Ira Meeks. I had known Ira since I was 14 years old and became his daughter's boyfriend. Ira was a rugged outdoorsman, a skilled hunter and the driver of an 18-wheel truck, piled high with hay. He taught me how to shoot a high-powered rifle, took me on hunting trips where we camped out under the stars and let me drive his great truck. Then, he changed. First, he would only stay in his own neighborhood, then his own backyard. In time, he had to be confined to a memory care facility. He lost all dignity and we lost him to the forest of confusion that is Alzheimer's disease.

Fifteen years after his death, my wife, June, began to show signs of memory loss. It was our grown children who urged me to have her memory tested. It turned out she did, indeed, have the beginnings of memory impairment. Over the past seven years, it has progressed to a full diagnosis of Alzheimer's. Our grandchildren and great grandchildren now have a Grandma who forgets.

Our hope rests in the work of Dr. Pierre Tariot and the staff at the Banner Alzheimer's Institute in Phoenix, AZ. June is receiving an experimental drug that appears able to dissolve the brain plaques that are the signature of Alzheimer's. It is possible that the progression of her disease can be halted in time.

It has been an honor and privilege to have some small part in this book with Maryann Makekau, who has done so much for children and their families through her Little Pink Book™ series.

June has always been my hero as she conquered many of life's greatest challenges. This fight is the toughest of all. I am in awe of her awareness, even of being unaware, and her determination to not give in.

Bob Deits

"Fighting Alzheimer's is like trying to punch out a cloud."
- June Deits

# TABLE OF CONTENTS

Chapter one
STUCK LIKE GLUE

Chapter two
FINDERS AND KEEPERS

Chapter three
LIBRARY VOICES, PLEASE

Chapter four
SOME-TIMERS AND ALL-TIMERS

Chapter five
PRETENDING AND THE REAL DEAL

Chapter six
CATCHING GRANDSHOTS

Chapter seven
WEEP WITH THOSE WHO WEEP

Chapter eight
MIRACLES OF HOPE

Chapter nine
LIFE MARCHES ON

Chapter ten
TIPS FOR CAREGIVERS

Resources

Keepers Journal

# STUCK LIKE GLUE

To understand Alzheimer's, it's important to know some facts about your brain. Your brain is like a puzzle. The parts fit together so well that it's like one part hugs another. Did you know that your brain weighs about three pounds? It weighs about the same as a carton of milk!

Inside your brain there are special cells called "neurons." You have about 100 billion neurons inside your brain, which is about the same number of stars in our galaxy! Your brain even has super powers—it creates enough electricity to make a light bulb shine bright!

The neurons in your brain send messages to your body so you can do things like get dressed, think, write, talk, walk, shower, cook and more. But sometimes diseases like Alzheimer's get in the way of the brain doing all its usual amazing work.

Saying the word "Alzheimer's" can be really hard! It's easier if you break the word into pieces: Allts—high—merz. When the brain gets Alzheimer's, it sort of looks like puzzle pieces glued together. The "glue" of Alzheimer's is called "plaques." That glue stops neurons from being able to send their messages. So, when your Grandma has Alzheimer's, she may have trouble talking, writing, remembering, and playing.

Sometimes medicines can keep the glue (plaques) from sticking. Doctors are also working on medicines that might wipe out the "glue." When medicine and miracles fit together like that it's like having a perfect puzzle inside your brain—which would be a big help to people with Alzheimer's.

Learning more about Alzheimer's is one of the best ways you and your family can help your Grandma cope with it. Coping means you get through something even if you can't change it. Nobody can change the fact that your Grandma has Alzheimer's, and no one caused her to get it either, but everyone can be part of helping, doing and sharing so that everyone can cope.

It's really important to ask questions and talk about feelings when someone you love is sick. Family, friends, doctors, nurses and other caregivers can all help. And remember, it's not contagious either—you can't catch Alzheimer's like a cold. So snuggle up for story-time and share lots of hugs with your Grandma!

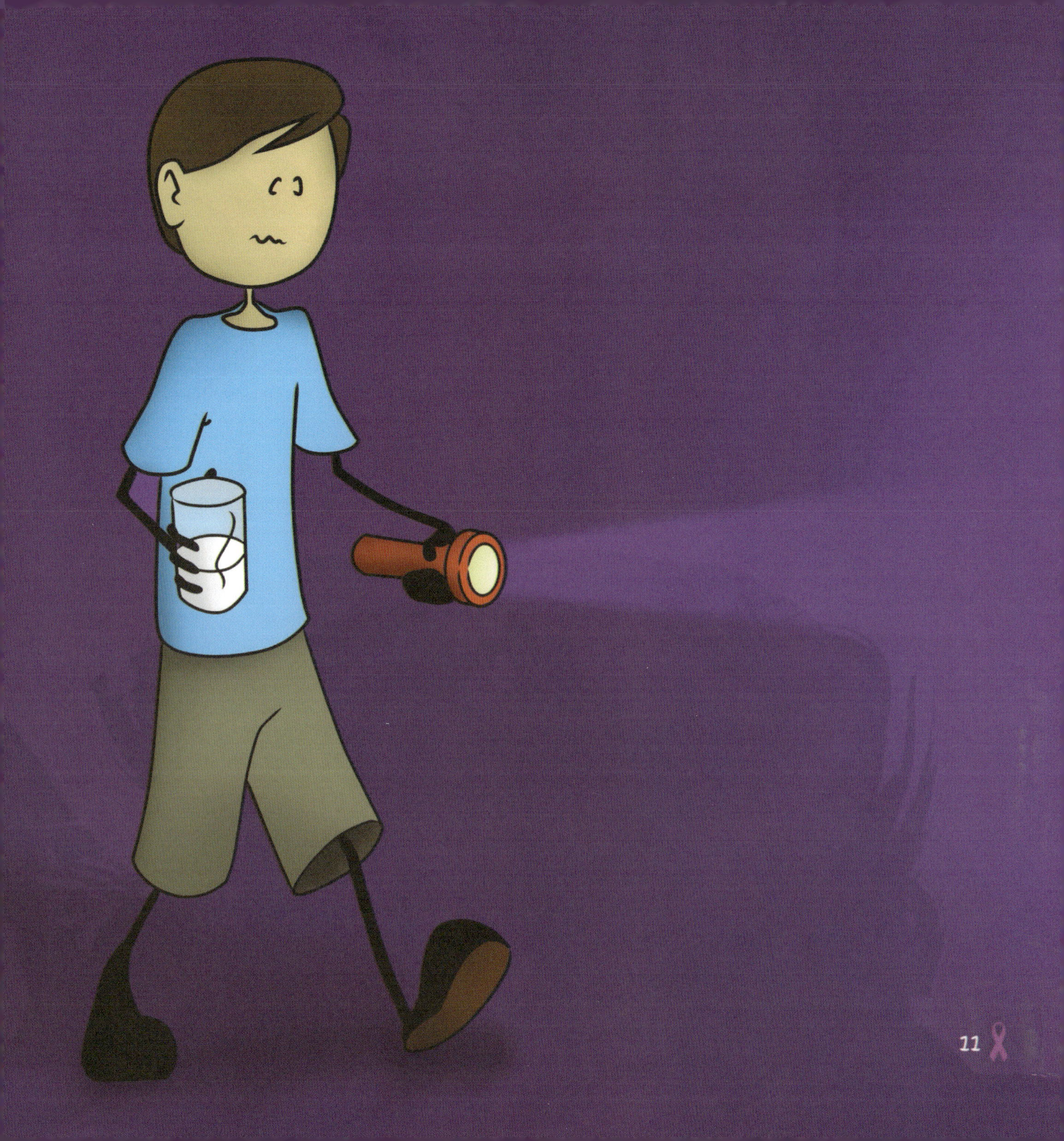

12

# FINDERS AND KEEPERS

Remember playing the game of "hide and seek?" You know the person you're looking for, but sometimes it's super hard to find them! Sometimes your Grandma just can't find the words she's looking for.

It's like her brain is playing hide-and-seek! She knows what she wants to say, but she can't seem to find the words. She might have to ask for your name or she might even call you by someone else's name! She might remember your name one minute and then forget it the next. But she never forgets the love for you she has tucked inside her heart.

You can help your Grandma by being one of her "finders." When she says the wrong word, ask her if you can help her find the right one. If she can't remember the word, whisper it to her so she can say it herself! When she calls you by a different name, just tell her your real name. Even if you told her two days ago or two minutes ago, it's okay to tell her again. You can just pretend it's the first time again!

Another way you can help your Grandma is by writing in a "keepers" journal. Keepers are special things you want to remember about your Grandma forever! You can write about things you and Grandma have done together. You can draw pictures in your journal, too. If you and your Grandma share a favorite prayer, that can go in there, too! If Grandma is having a hard day, you can remind her of favorite things by sharing your Keepers journal. Everyone should have a list of Keepers like that!

# LIBRARY VOICES, PLEASE!

Have you ever had a really big birthday party? Inviting lots of friends, playing games and running around can be super fun! Your birthday is really important to your Grandma, but she might need to celebrate with you in a different way. Noisy places can be very confusing and even scary for her. So, you might want to have a quiet party at her house after your noisy party with friends. And what kid doesn't want to have two birthday parties?

You can also help your Grandma by asking everyone to take turns talking. When people take turns, they're practicing good manners, and that's always helpful. When it gets too noisy for your Grandma, remind everyone to use their "library voices." Everyone knows that libraries are places where people do everything quietly!

Another way to help your Grandma is by giving her extra time to answer your questions. As that glue called "plaques" spreads inside her brain, it gets harder for her to talk. It's like having to tell your brain to "get unstuck" so the words can come out of your mouth! Let your Grandma try to come up with the words by herself before you help out. It'll make her happy to do things on her own, and she'll be very thankful for your patience.

PARTY #2

15

16

# SOME-TIMERS AND ALL-TIMERS

There's a big difference between "some-timers" and "all-timers." Some-timers happen to everyone, even kids! When you get to school and realize you forgot your lunch money or your homework, that's a "some-timers" moment! You don't have that kind of moment everyday, just sometimes. It's normal for everyone to forget sometimes. It's also normal to forget some things completely, like you probably can't remember being a baby now that you're a big kid!

When someone has Alzheimer's though, they have lots of "some-timers." As the disease gets worse, your Grandma's forgetful moments are more like "all-timers." She forgets things all the time, instead of just sometimes.

She might forget what you told her last week, yesterday or even a minute ago. She might forget how to button her shirt or how to put on her seatbelt. She might forget how to write or how to take a bath. She might forget to lean over her plate, and then food ends up on her lap or on the floor. She might even forget that she's hungry, and family has to remind her that it's time to eat.

She might forget how to use the bathroom and end up in a stinky mess—that's a super embarrassing moment! And then she might get stuck in there because she forgets how to unlock the door. So, caregivers like your Grandpa, your mom or a friend, will need to be very kind and patient about helping your Grandma get unstuck from such embarrassing moments.

Sometimes, you might feel sad knowing that your Grandma is forgetting important things like where she is, how to use the bathroom, your name, or even her own name. That's when everyone needs to remember that humor is medicine, too. When Grandma tries to turn on the television with the cordless phone—have a good laugh together! When she puts a candy wrapper in the dishwasher, just smile as you give it the right home in the trashcan!

Hang loose—don't stress about what you can't fix. Instead, watch a funny movie, write in your "keepers" journal, and remind your Grandpa to invite another caregiver over so he can go play golf. Go for a manicure with your Mom and Grandma for some girl-time. Say "I love you," hug each other, and do fun things together!

# PRETENDING AND THE REAL DEAL

Have you ever had a really, really bad day? Maybe your teacher heard you call your friend that not-so-nice name, and now you're in trouble with your friend and your teacher! My, oh my, how did you get into such a pickle?

Everyone has a bad day from time to time. You might get upset and not want to talk about it because you feel ashamed or embarrassed. Saying "I'm sorry" is the right thing to do, but it's not always so easy.

With Alzheimer's, your Grandma might not remember when she does something wrong. Or she might be too embarrassed to admit it. She's not going to remember or admit to being wrong because you argue with her about it! Arguing can be embarrassing and hurtful, especially when your Grandma can't say all the words she wishes she could. If your Grandma says she forgot, then she forgot. Arguing just makes everyone grouchy!

Yet, sometimes her behavior can seem so unfair. If she loses something, she might yell at you and even think you stole it! Then when she finds it or your Grandpa finds it—she has a hard time accepting the "real deal." She might say that it never even happened! That kind of behavior can hurt other people's feelings. Forgive your Grandma even when she seems to be pretending or won't accept the real deal. It's always better to forgive than to stay mad about things.

Sometimes people with Alzheimer's curse—you know, those bad words you shouldn't ever say! Or your Grandma might behave in very embarrassing ways. Remember how neurons control your body? Well, they also control your behavior. You've probably heard your teacher tell a noisy student to "check your behavior!" Alzheimer's creates big problems for your Grandma and all those who love her because she can't always "check" her behavior. That's the real deal about living with Alzheimer's.

19

# CATCHING GRANDSHOTS

While Alzheimer's can make it hard for your Grandma to remember what happened yesterday, it might be easy for her to remember what happened many years ago. That might not make sense, but it's often the way it is with Alzheimer's.

You can have some fun with your Grandma by looking into the past together. Take out those old family albums and look at all the memories inside. Ask her to tell you stories about her childhood and all the people she's met. You can have a camera handy for new snapshots, too. Pictures taken with your Grandma are extra special—they're "Grandshots!"

You can have Grandshots of birthday parties, holiday meals, music recitals, soccer games, and vacations. There are other ways to collect Grandshots, too. Your mom might have a Facebook page where she shares special moments with family. Your sister might have a Keepers journal. Your brother might keep a special box with rocks he's collected from camping trips.

Time spent together is another very special Grandshot! You and your Grandma can play favorite music and sing together, watch a favorite television show together, paint a picture, or make a beaded necklace together.

Moments filled with laughter are great Grandshots, too. Like when your family is sitting around the dinner table and your sister's funny story makes your Grandma burst out laughing. Or when you're singing together and, all of a sudden, you're both dancing in your seats! Although those kinds of moments may not be as often as before, they're definitely Grandshots to catch. No matter how hard it is watching your Grandma go through Alzheimer's, you can always find special moments to treasure!

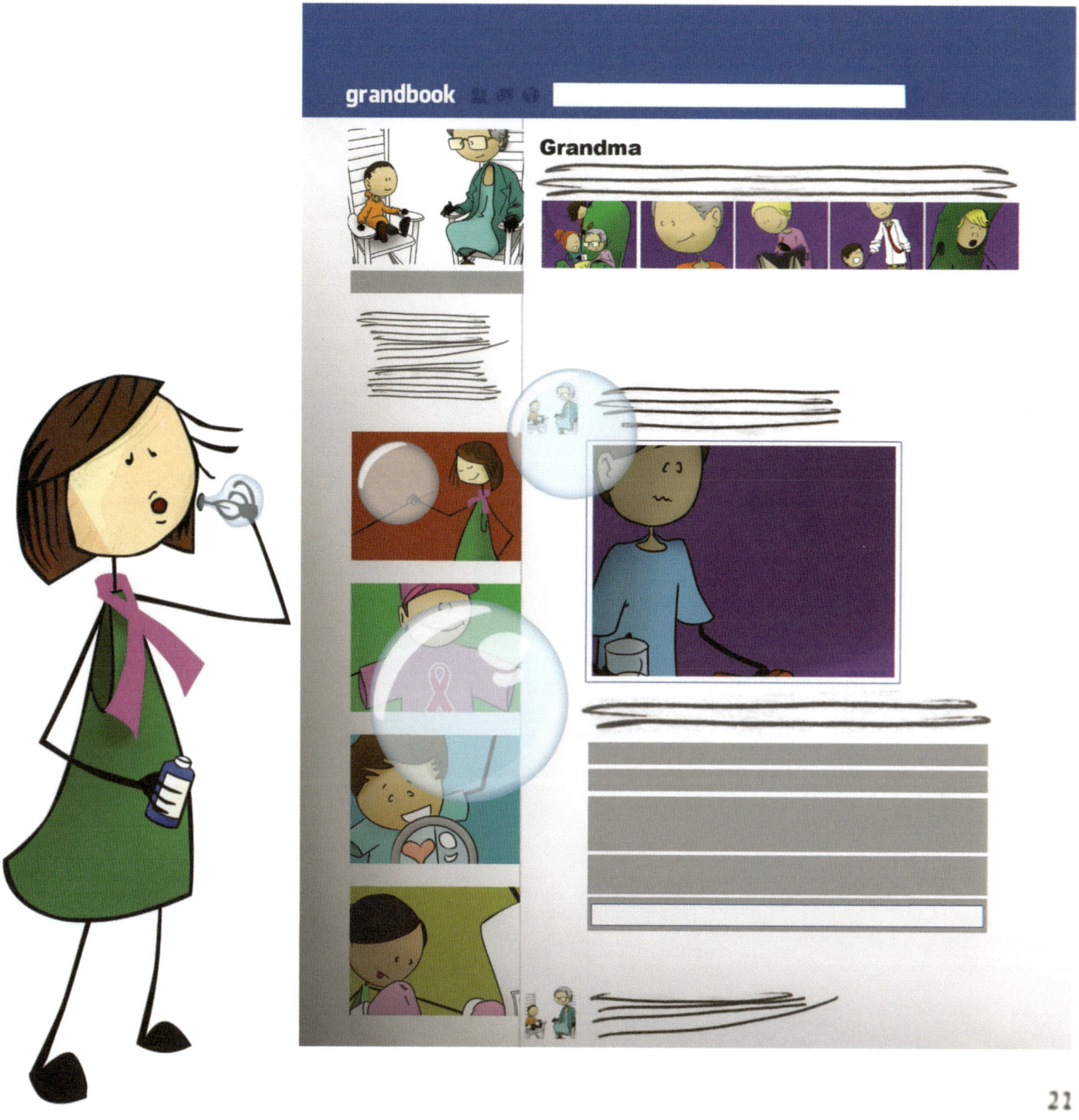
grandbook
Grandma

# WEEP WITH THOSE WHO WEEP

Knowing your Grandma has Alzheimer's can cause you and your family to have a lot of different feelings. It's sad for everyone who loves her because they miss the way Grandma used to be. It's good to weep with those who weep—crying helps the ache in your heart and makes you feel better.

You might feel nervous when you don't know if it's a good day or a bad day for Grandma. It might frighten you to hear your Grandpa talk about putting extra locks on the doors for safety or that your Grandma might have to live in a new place. Share your feelings with your mom, dad, Grandpa or your teacher—or you may end up sadder, more afraid and mad.

happy          sad          angry

Sometimes people even get foot-stomping, screaming mad at Alzheimer's! They might yell at God when their prayers to make Grandma better don't get answered! It's okay to get really mad like that sometimes. It's hard to understand why your Grandma has Alzheimer's. Why can't the doctors make it go away? Why can't the medicines fix it? Why is everything about taking care of Grandma? What happened to having fun together?

Repeating yourself is no fun either. When your Grandpa tells your Grandma over and over what time dinner will be served, he might lose his temper. Seeing your Grandpa angry might make you get angry, too!

Even if your Grandma can't find the words to say it—she's frustrated, angry and sad, too. Having Alzheimer's is a lot like trying to punch a cloud. If you punched a cloud, your arm would go right through it; and the cloud wouldn't change shape at all! There's no way to punch through the cloud of confusion inside your Grandma's brain, and that's one of the most frustrating things about Alzheimer's. No matter what you do to help or what medicines your Grandma takes, Alzheimer's is chronic—it's not going away!

scared         frustrated         confused

But Alzheimer's can't take hope away! Hope lives in your heart and can be more helpful than medicine when someone you love is sick. You can share your hope in lots of ways. Make a habit of watching funny movies, making jokes, being silly, playing outside, stargazing together, and sharing lots of hugs. Be patient with your Grandma—it helps her cope with having Alzheimer's. Remind her that she's very special to you, and tell her often, "I love you, Grandma!"

# MIRACLES OF HOPE

Sometimes medicines lead to miracles and the people we love get better. But other times, medicines are only helpful for awhile and Alzheimer's gets much worse. It's easy to forget about hope when your Grandma doesn't recognize you, your Grandpa or your Mom. The longer your Grandma lives with Alzheimer's, the bigger the cloud of confusion becomes. Then she doesn't even get out of bed, talk, sing or laugh anymore.

Seeing your Grandma like this is scary, frustrating and sad—all at the same time. Everyone in your family feels different things and that gets very confusing, too. Some people might smile and say "she won't have to put up with Alzheimer's in Heaven!"

But hope still makes good things happen. Hope lets you still celebrate every moment you visit your Grandma. Hope lets you tell her funny stories because she can still listen, even if she doesn't talk. Hope lets you still share special Grandshots. Hope reminds you to say, "I love you" and "you're so special, Grandma." And hope reminds you that Heaven is a place where there are no more tears and no more Alzheimer's!

Not everyone dies from Alzheimer's, but sometimes that does happen. When medicines can't give your Grandma's memory a boost anymore and the glue-like plaques can't be erased, she'll get too tired to keep fighting. The neurons don't send messages anymore—then her body and organs quit working. Even the doctors can't fix everything.

That's when love becomes the only super power—for everyone who has to say good-bye to your Grandma. Love is someone putting a warm blanket on her when the room feels chilly. Love is someone brushing her hair very gently. Love is someone holding her hand.

When your Grandma sleeps a lot, you can still give her kisses. She may not talk about your kisses, but she'll store them in her heart! Share Grandshot moments and laughter when visiting with your Grandma instead of worry and fear. She'll be grateful to be surrounded by the miracles called hope and love.

25

# LIFE MARCHES ON

When someone you love dies, it can be hard to talk about it. Sometimes adults try to say helpful things like, "at least she won't suffer anymore and she's in Heaven now." Or "she had a good, long life." None of those sayings make it easier. In fact, you might feel really mad hearing them! If you're eight, you've only had eight years with her—so to you, her life didn't feel long at all!

People say those things because they're trying to help. But it's really the simple things that help the most. Hugs and "I love you's" can help more when you're sad, angry, confused, and scared all at the same time! Grief is a sadness that everyone feels—no matter how old they are! As people share their grief at a memorial service—they'll cry because they're sad, but they'll also laugh about the great Grandshots. Remember, laughter is God's best medicine—even in the saddest moments!

So what happens after someone you love dies? What does it look like when life marches on? If your Grandpa spent every day taking care of your Grandma, his life will change a lot. If your mom or dad did a lot for your Grandma, their life will change too. Not having your Grandma around can feel like there's a big hole in your lives—and in your hearts. You can fill that hole by sharing your feelings. Everyone will have sad days and, at first, there may be a lot of sad days. Later, your Grandma's birthday, holidays, and other special occasions might make your family feel sad all over again.

The best way to feel better when you lose someone you love is to remember that life does march on! Your Grandma would want everyone to keep playing, working and celebrating together. You have to go back to school, do your chores and play with your friends. Your parents have to go to work and do things that make them smile and have fun. Maybe your Grandpa will start doing things he didn't have time for before, like playing golf or going fishing. Everyone needs to march on with life while carrying Grandma's love in their hearts.

You can still celebrate her birthday—your family can get together for a meal and share Grandshots! If you know someone who's good at sewing, your Grandma's t-shirts could be made into an awesome quilt. Then every time you use that special blanket, you'll be covered with Grandma's love! You can plant a tree in the yard with your Grandpa and as it grows you'll have a constant reminder of how pretty and strong your Grandma was.

Losing someone you love is always hard. Knowing they went to Heaven helps the pain in your heart, but you never stop missing them. When missing your Grandma hurts, let your mom, dad or Grandpa know. Share your love, lots of hugs, prayers, and "Grandshots." With faith, hope and love, life marches on in amazing ways!

27

# TIPS FOR CAREGIVERS

1. Remember that the woman you knew is still inside the one you see now.

2. What's happening inside a brain with Alzheimer's is similar to pouring glue inside a computer—once it hardens (like plaques) it is "stuck like glue."

3. Let go of opinions and expectations of what's acceptable for your loved one or for you to do. Be ready to lay out clothes, help her get dressed (even her underwear), cut up her food, and place needed utensils in her hand. Use napkins and bibs to protect her clothing. Be humbly ready to give step-by-step directions for bathing or using the toilet; have latex gloves and moist wipes on-hand.

4. If your loved one with Alzheimer's lives with you, expect frequent interruptions to your sleep. Consider safety measures if she tends to turn on stove burners or wander off (see Readings & Resources).

5. Help your loved one feel useful as her capacity to do things increasingly diminishes. Quietly adjust the table settings when something's awry—avoid pointing out errors. Encourage her to continue tasks like unloading the dishwasher or folding clothes.

6. Keep life routine as much as possible and space out activities so that your loved one doesn't get overwhelmed. Share plans on the day they are to take place; this prevents anticipatory anxiety.

7. Be responsible for your loved one's medications. Observe her taking medications, making sure she takes them as prescribed (e.g. chewed vs. swallowed with water).

8. Help your loved one dress in clothes that are attractive—consider her favorite colors and styles. Consider slip-on shoes that are easier to put on.

9. If your loved one enjoys eating out, do that on a regular basis and guide healthy food choices. Review menu items ahead of time if possible; this lessens confusion for her in busy restaurants.

10. Remember to take time out—caregivers need to be cared for, too!

# RESOURCES

## HELPFUL READS:

- *Alzheimer's from the Inside Out* by Richard Taylor
- *The Complete Eldercare Planner: Where to Start, Questions to Ask, How to Find Help* by Joy Loverde
- *The 36-Hour Day* by Nancy L. Mace, M.A. and Peter V. Rabins, M.D., M.P.H.
- *My Mother, Your Mother* by Dennis McCullough MD

## HELPFUL SITES:

- Alzheimer's Foundation of America
- Banner Alzheimer's Institute
- MedicAlert® + Alzheimer's Association Safe Return®
- Alzheimer's Disease Education and Referral (ADEAR) Center
- Caregivers Home Companion

## REFERENCES USED FOR THIS PUBLICATION:

- *Alzheimer's from the Inside Out* by Richard Taylor
- Neuroscience for Kids: http://faculty.washington.edu/chudler/what.html
- American Association of Retired Persons: http://www.aarp.org/

# KEEPERS JOURNAL

Printed in Great Britain
by Amazon

77533163R00018